D0859682

READY, SET, DRAW!

CARS, TRUCKS, AND MOTORCYCLES YOU CAN DRAW

Nicole Brecke

Patricia M. Stockland

M Millbrook Press / Minneapolis

Edited by Mari Kesselring
Research by Emily Temple

Millbrook Press
A division of Lerner Publishing Group, Inc.
241 First Avenue North
Minneapolis, MN 55401 U.S.A.

Website address: www.lernerbooks.com

Library of Congress Cataloging-in-Publication Data

Brecke, Nicole.
        Cars, trucks, and motorcycles you can draw / by Nicole Brecke and Patricia M. Stockland ;
    illustrations by Nicole Brecke.
                p.   cm. — (Ready, set, draw!)
            Includes index.
            ISBN: 978-0-7613-4162-8 (lib. bdg. : alk. paper)
                1. Automobiles in art—Juvenile literature. 2. Trucks in art—Juvenile literature.
        3. Motorcycles in art—Juvenile literature. 4. Drawing—Technique—Juvenile literature.
        I. Stockland, Patricia M. II. Title.
        NC825.A8B74 2010
        743'.8962922—dc22   2009002581

Manufactured in the United States of America
2 – BP – 4/1/10

TABLE OF CONTENTS

ABOUT THIS BOOK

Drive it. Race it. Jump it! Cars, trucks, and motorcycles are mega machines of fun. And drawing them is fun too. With the help of this book, you can begin sketching your favorites. Draw a semi. Color a dirt bike. Soon you'll know how to draw many different vehicles.

Follow these steps to create each machine. Each drawing begins with a basic form. The form is made up of a line and a shape or two. These lines and shapes will help you make your drawing the correct size.

A First, read all the steps and look at the pictures. Then use a pencil to lightly draw the line and shapes shown in RED. You will erase these lines later.

B Next, draw the lines shown in BLUE.

C Keep going! Once you have completed a step, the color of the line changes to BLACK. Follow the BLUE line until you're done.

WHAT YOU WILL NEED

PENCIL SHARPENER

COLORED PENCILS

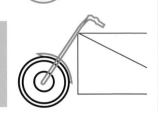

HELPFUL HINTS

Use your imagination. Get creative. Read about your favorite car, truck, or bike, and then follow the steps to create your own fleet of speed and power.

Practice drawing different lines and shapes. All of your drawings will start with these.

ERASER

Use very light pencil lines when you are drawing.

Helpful tips and hints will offer you good ideas on making the most of your sketch.

PENCIL

Colors are exciting. Try to use a variety of shades. This will add value, or depth, to your finished drawings.

PAPER

Keep practicing, and have fun!

HOW TO DRAW A CONVERTIBLE

Feel the wind in your hair. Feel the sun on your face. Take a ride in a convertible! Convertibles have been around for many years. The first convertibles came with tops that had to be closed by hand. Eventually, convertibles with motorized tops hit the market. Motorized tops made convertibles convenient—and even more fun—to drive. These days, convertibles are a sporty choice in cars. Many carmakers offer open tops on their favorite models. Put the top down, and go for a spin!

1 Lightly draw a long, skinny base rectangle. Add two base circles.

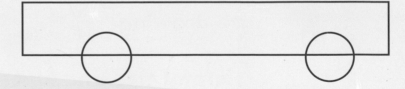

2

Starting at the right circle, draw the nose of the car. Stay inside the rectangle, and make the top and the back bumper. Add a fender above the left circle, and trace over the base circles to finish the wheels.

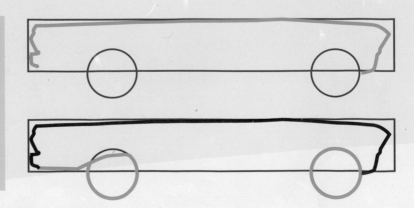

3 Draw the underbody. Add two vertical door lines. Make the windshield with two diagonal lines and two smaller horizontal lines. Add a short vertical line. Add a front bumper. Draw a small circle and a larger circle inside each wheel.

4 Carefully erase your extra baselines. Add details. Make a door handle, tire rims, a paint line, and a folded top.

5 Now it's time to color your convertible!

HOW TO DRAW A MONSTER TRUCK

What can jump distances of 115 feet (35 meters) and crush as many as twenty-five cars? Monster trucks! Wild paint jobs and super sizes make monster trucks a favorite at truck rallies. These massive machines also have monster names, such as Bigfoot, Grave Digger, and Blue Thunder. Grilles might look like teeth. And skulls and crossbones on a hood scare away the competition. Monster trucks are custom-made, so no two are alike. These beasts are ready to rumble and race.

1

Lightly draw a base rectangle and top line. Add two sets of three circles.

2

Draw the top of the hood, cab, box, tailgate, and bumper. Add two vertical door lines and a headlight.

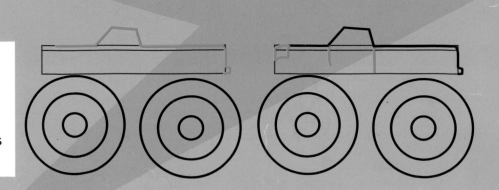

3 Add a horizontal line under the hood, cab, and box. Draw a roll bar and a window. Add a front bumper. Make a curved line above each tire. Connect them with a horizontal line.

4 Erase your extra lines. Draw four sets of shocks. Add two diagonal lines and a connecting horizontal line.

5 Now it's time to color your monster truck!

HOW TO DRAW A FERRARI

Sleek, sporty, and speedy all describe the Ferrari. This famous race car is a favorite among the rich and famous. Enzo Ferrari was the creator of these flashy speedsters. He started his own racing team called Scuderia Ferrari. This means "Ferrari's Stable." The Ferrari's logo is a prancing horse. It's a fitting symbol for a very fast car. Ferraris have a long history of winning races. With complicated, powerful engines, they easily outrace other cars. But Ferraris aren't cheap. A 1961 model sold for almost $11 million in 2008.

Draw a light base rectangle and center line. Add an oval and two angled lines. Connect the angled lines.

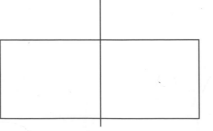

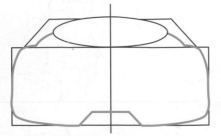

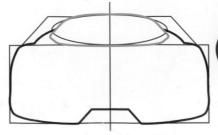

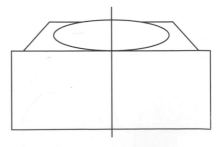

Starting at each side of the oval, draw curved lines inside the base rectangle to form the body. Add a windshield to the oval.

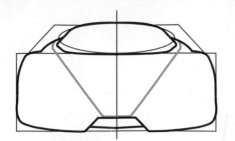

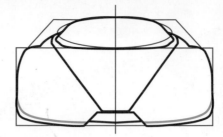

3

Draw two diagonal lines on the hood. Add two lines to the bottom.

4

Draw two more lines. Add rearview mirrors and a spoiler.

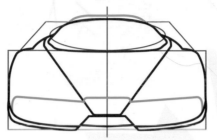

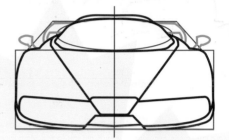

5

Carefully erase your extra baselines. Add headlights and hood and grille details.

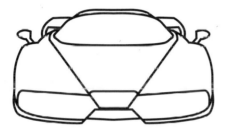

6 Now it's time to color your Ferrari!

HOW TO DRAW A DIRT BIKE

If you want a light, fast ride, then a dirt bike might be your machine. These bikes are actually small motorcycles. Dirt bikes are built for off-road racing. They have large, knobby tires and small, light engines. Dirt bike races are called motocross or supercross. These races are popular all around the world. And so are dirt bikes. Riders must tackle jumps, turns, and rough terrain. Dirt bike riders also need lots of safety gear. Padded suits, goggles, helmets, gloves, and more protect these racers.

1

Lightly draw a box and a diagonal baseline. Add a small circle and then a medium and large circle to make a wheel. Repeat circles.

2

Use the baseline to make a long, skinny rectangle. Add two lines starting from the smallest circle on the left. Join the lines with a short vertical line on one side.

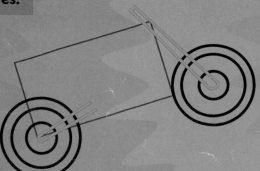

3 Add a fender to the front of the bike. Draw a handlebar. Follow the top of the base square to make the seat and back fender.

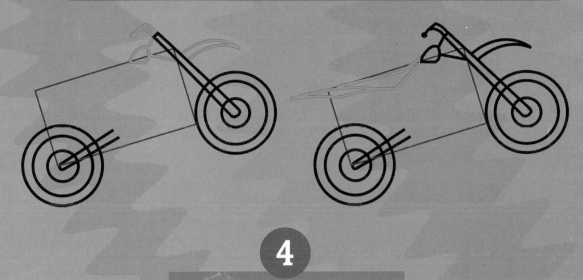

4

Draw the back of the engine. Add the motor and gas tank.

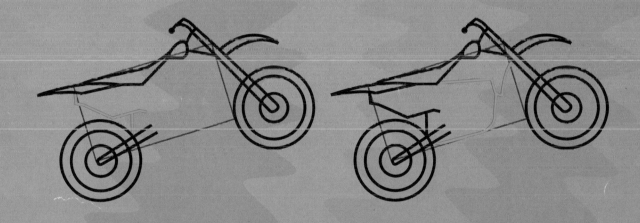

5 Draw two curved vertical lines. Connect these on the gas tank. Add a small circle for the gearshift.

7

Erase the wheel lines that fall inside the frame.

Did you know...

DIRT BIKES NEED LIGHTS TO BE STREET LEGAL.

Some dirt bike courses have hills, streams, bogs, and rocky terrain.

8 Now it's time to color your dirt bike!

MAKE MUD

Add different shades of brown spots to show mud.

HOW TO DRAW A SEMITRUCK

Want a hardworking, heavy-duty truck? Then you need a semitruck. This transportation giant was built to haul big loads across long distances. Semitrucks move everything from livestock to living-room furniture. Semis are also known as big rigs. Some big rigs are shiny with chrome. Others have full-size beds that drivers call home. That's right—they can sleep in their parked trucks! There are lots of specialized haulers out there with extra exhaust pipes and extra power. Watch the road for your favorite freight mover.

1 Draw a light base rectangle with a middle baseline. Add a square. Draw the top half of the trailer on the top half of the rectangle.

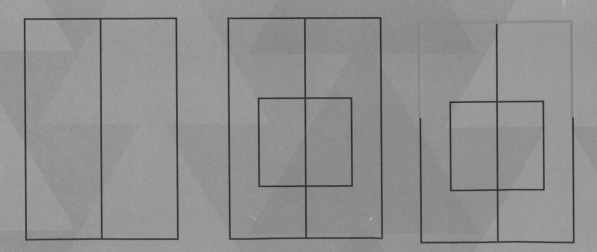

2

Add a slightly curved rectangle to make the top half of the cab. Draw two small curving lines off each end. Outline the smaller box. Add a windshield and vertical grille lines.

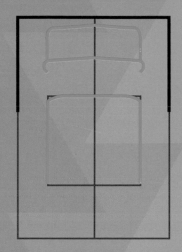

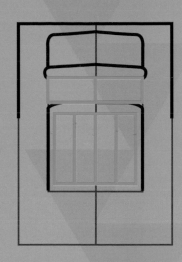

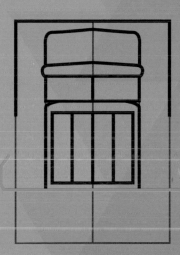

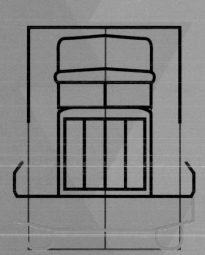

3

Draw two curved lines connected by a horizontal line. Add the front bumper and two tires.

Lots of Tires...

SEMITRUCKS
ARE ALSO
CALLED
EIGHTEEN-WHEELERS.

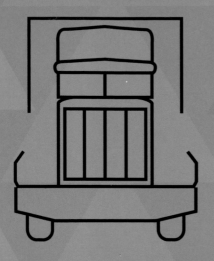

4 Carefully erase any extra baselines.

5 Add two vertical lines and four small diagonal lines to finish the cab. Draw a horseshoe shape and a small rectangle for each fender.

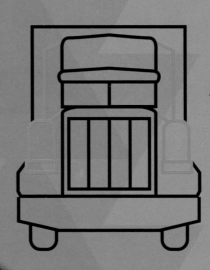

NICE RIG

Some drivers like to deck out their trucks. Make your truck shine.

DRAW STACKS AND MIRRORS!

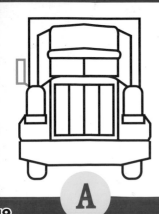

A

B

C

SEMITRUCKS use air brakes for extra stopping power when hauling heavy loads.

6 Now it's time to color your semitruck!

HOW TO DRAW A JEEP

The popular Jeep was introduced in the 1940s. The U.S. Army asked engineers to create a small, powerful vehicle to use during war combat. Soldiers liked the Jeep so much that it soon went on sale to the public. Jeeps are compact, sturdy, and built to go off-road. Some people belong to Jeep clubs. These groups take road trips. Some owners rebuild old Jeeps. And others make special changes to their trucks. These Jeeps are customized. Tough tires, super shocks, and strong suspension all make a well-built Jeep.

1

Lightly draw a base box and an angled center line. Add two ovals for tires and a rectangle for the windshield. Draw a line outside the rectangle to form the top.

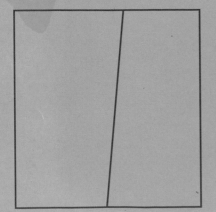
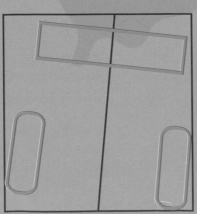
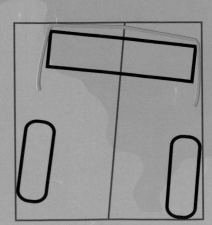

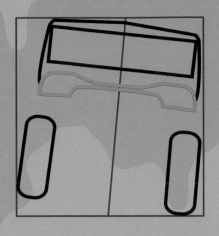

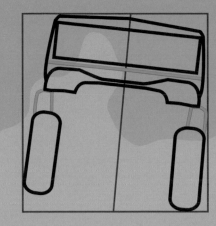

2 Add a curved hood. Draw a line under the windshield. Use two lines to connect each tire to the hood.

3 Draw a horizontal line above the two tires. Add a curved line underneath. Connect the tires with a line and two half circles. Add rearview mirrors.

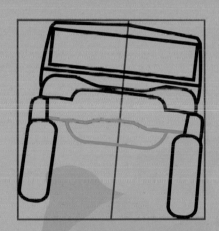

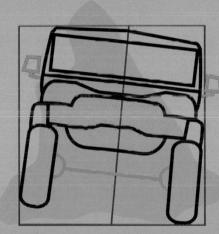

Did you know...

THERE ARE AREAS AND PARKS USED SPECIFICALLY FOR JEEP TRAIL DRIVING.

4

Draw two circles for headlights. Add two smaller circles for fog lights and two small rectangles for blinkers.

5 Carefully erase your base box and center line.

MANY JEEPS are sold with removable tops. This makes them a sort of all-terrain convertible.

6

Draw five tall, skinny ovals between the headlights for the grille.

A Jeep ride
is a great way
to see the
outdoors.

7

Now it's time to color your Jeep!

HOW TO DRAW A MOTORCYCLE

Power and two wheels make a motorcycle. These fast machines were first built in 1885 in Germany. Since then, motorcycles have gained fans around the world. Rallies, rides, and races are all popular motorcycling events. Riders like the freedom and speed of cycling. They also enjoy the different makes and models of motorcycles. Harley Davidson, Honda, Yamaha, and BMW all design popular bikes. Safety is important when driving or riding a motorcycle. Don't forget long sleeves, pants, eyewear, sturdy boots—and a helmet.

1 Draw a light base rectangle. Add a diagonal line to the inside and another line to the outside.

2 Add two sets of three circles for the wheels.

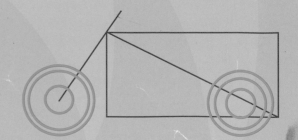

3

Add a second parallel line to the front of the frame, and connect it to the other line at the bottom. Trace over the other line. Draw a fender over the wheel. Add a handlebar. Draw a gas tank and a seat inside the base rectangle.

4

Draw another fender behind the seat, over the back wheel. Make an L shape along the bottom of the rectangle. Add two more curved L shapes inside this.

5

Under the gas tank, add two small angled lines. Draw two curved horizontal lines for the exhaust pipe. Add a headlight and a cable line (a small cord that connects controls to the handlebar).

6 Carefully erase your base shape and center line.

7 Erase the extra wheel lines inside your frame and exhaust pipe.

UNIQUE RIDE

Custom-built motorcycles are called choppers.

DRAW A FLAME PAINT JOB!

A

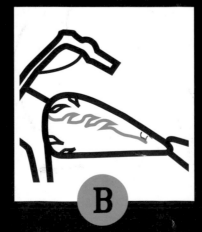

B

C

In 1904, the first Harley Davidson motorcycle was introduced.

8 Now it's time to color your motorcycle!

The first Sturgis Motorcycle Rally was held in 1938, in Sturgis, South Dakota.

HOW TO DRAW AN INDY CAR

Indy cars are open-wheel race cars. Open-wheel race cars are made to move. Indy cars are a favorite type of open wheeler, with lean, aerodynamic lines that help the car go even faster. Like other open-wheel race cars, Indy cars do not have fenders over the tires. Winning an open-wheel race is all about skill and speed. Fans have followed these historic machines for years. Drivers such as Mario Andretti, A. J. Foyt, and Danica Patrick have helped make open-wheel racing famous around the world.

1 Lightly draw a base box and center line. Add two more base rectangles, one to each side.

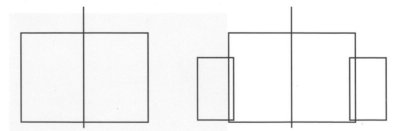

2 Use the smaller rectangles to outline the wheels. Draw a dented horizontal line across the bottom to connect the wheels.

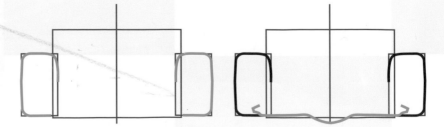

28

3 Draw a curved line at the top corners of the base box. Add a zigzag line under the curved line, on the inside of each wheel.

4 Make a sideways L shape above each zigzag line. In the center, draw a tall vase shape. Add two short lines to the bottom of this.

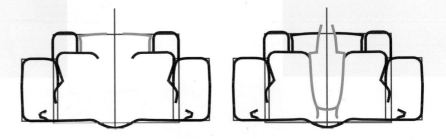

5 Draw another horizontal line across the bottom. Add a shorter horizontal line to each side above the long line and connect them to the long line. Make three short lines.

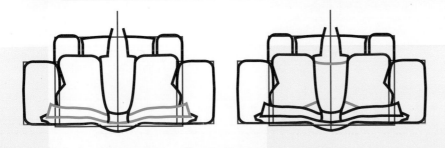

6 Add a small circle and a T shape to the top of the cockpit. Draw three horizontal lines on each side of this for the wings. Make a small vertical line on each end to connect the wings to the car.

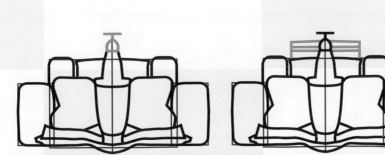

7 Carefully erase any extra baselines.

8

Draw two rounded squares for headlights. Add a small rectangle to the nose.

READY TO RACE

Create excitement for your Indy car by sketching in some details.

DRAW A DRIVER AND A NUMBER!

A

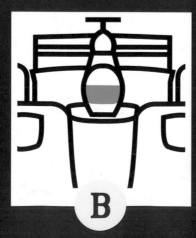

B

C

9 Now it's time to color your Indy car!

FURTHER READING

Cars That Think
http://www.pbs.org/saf/1502

Collision Kids
http://www.collisionkids.org

Dubosque, Doug. *Draw 3-D: A Step-by-Step Guide to Perspective Drawing*. Columbus, NC: Peel Productions, 1998.

Dubowski, Mark. *Superfast Motorcycles*. New York: Bearport, 2006.

Ferrari Website
http://www.ferrariworld.com/FWorld/fw/index.jsp

Stewart, Mark, and Mike Kennedy. *NASCAR at the Track*. Minneapolis: Lerner Publications Company, 2008.

Zobel, Derek. *Monster Vehicles*. Minneapolis: Bellwether Media, 2008.

INDEX